Sin Is Due to Open in a Room Above Kitty's

Morag Anderson

First published August 2021
Published in the UK by Fly on the Wall Press
56 High Lea Rd, New Mills, Derbyshire, SK22 3DP

www.flyonthewallpress.co.uk
Copyright Morag Anderson © 2021
ISBN: 978-1-913211-59-2

The right of Morag Anderson to be identified as the author of this work has been asserted in accordance with the Copyright, Designs and Patents Act 1988.
Typesetting by Isabelle Kenyon. Cover photo from Unsplash.

All rights reserved. No part of this publication may be reproduced, stored in or introduced into a retrieval system, or transmitted in any form, or by any means (electronic, mechanical, photocopying, recording or otherwise) without prior written permissions of the publisher. Any person who does any unauthorised act in relation to this publication may be liable for criminal prosecution and civil claims for damages. A CIP Catalogue record for this book is available from the British Library.

For R and 3Js

Notes:

Sin is Due to Open in a Room Above Kitty's. The title is adapted from a newspaper article in The Courier newspaper, October 2018. *A Thirst for Rain.* First line is attributable to Rosemary Tonks' 'The Sofas, Fogs, and Cinemas'.

Acknowledgements:

Thanks are due to the editors of the following publications in which some of these poems, or versions of them, have previously appeared: *Finished Creatures, The Broken Spine Arts Collective, Popshot Quarterly, The Scotsman, Skylight 47, Laldy!, The Darg, The Blue Nib, High Tide (FWS), Postcards from Malthusia, A Plague of Poetry.*

Much gratitude is due to the following people: my friend, poet, and mentor Audrey Molloy for the gift of encouragement, time, and her keen poetic eye; Maeve O'Reilly McKenna, Jo Burns, Barbara DeCoursey Roy, Bobbie Sparrow, Anne Walsh Donnelly, and Attracta Fahy for helping me find my voice; Kevin Higgins, who inspired many of these poems through his *Over the Edge* poetry workshops; Jim Mackintosh and Jon Plunkett, poets and friends, for opening the door to poetry.

Without the constancy of his love and the gift of space, none of this would be possible—Ross, thank you.

Contents

Two Doors Down	6
The Heated Kitchen	7
Paterfamilias	8
What I Remember of Your Tongue	9
Offertory	10
Last Supper with Sarah	11
Spotlight	13
Sin Is Due to Open in a Room Above Kitty's	14
Two Things I Know, Father Byrne	15
What It Means to Prey	16
A Thirst for Rain	17
A Seed Sown	18
After Work Drinks, Holborn	19
Cherries	20
New Year	21
The Mistake I Always Make	22
She Is Plotting Against Me	23
Shaping Words	24
The Mathematics of Chance	25
DNR	26
Glasgow Coma Scale	27
Killing Time in the Relatives' Room	28
Kintsugi	29
In the School of Life Sciences	30
Orkney	32
I Was Once a Girl in a Fountain, Splashing a Boy	33

Two Doors Down

He conjured coins
from Sunday-scrubbed ears
or the King of Clubs
from hems of skirt
—daftest Dad on our street.

But when sleep
snuffed his household
he slunk
from stagnant sheets,
placed a hesitant hand
upon the door's rose
and crossed the lilac carpet
to finger
the pink candlewick.

Choosing to believe
in space created
by the child,
rigid against ponies
papered to her wall,
he slid in.

But when truth
awoke his household
he shrunk
inside his bleeding brain,
was left too dead
to repent.

No-one collected his ashes.
They believe
he is burning yet.

The Heated Kitchen

But for the surge of colour your fist brought to my cheek
reflected in the specular drop at the tap's mouth;

the tang of coins warm on my bloodied tongue
amplifying the tick of the cooling heater;

the twist of hair in throttled gesticulation
unravelling the thrum of voices next door;

the broken doll blink of my eyelid
rasping faint as a distant dog

the slurry of words spewing your whisky haar
scorching the sweetness of blackened bananas;

and the smothered sobs bonding sternum to spine
drowning the bell-curve pitch of a passing siren,

it was an ordinary day.

Paterfamilias

When the breadth of your back
is no more than narrative
beneath the tailored twill of your shirt,

when your fingers, gone to driftwood,
rattle and clack against the ancestral
crest of old gold,

when you cannot rise to greet
the changing seasons that slant
across your vaulted ceiling,

when cataracts cloud the sky
and your intended ascension
seems less assured,

may your daughters labour with language,
give birth to books that punctuate
the end of your line.

What I Remember of Your Tongue

The bird that lives in woods
behind my house, breaks
my sleep with song,
serves no joy or truth.

The bat that drops at dusk
from resting beams
above my head, reveals
an underbelly of rust.

The fire's stalking smoke
clings to my skin,
freights muted lungs
with its shapeless choke.

The disconnected tone,
F-sharp flatlining,
when impulse dials
your pulseless red phone.

Offertory

Day streams through the drama
of stained glass.
Light animates dust,
imparts colour in cobalt blue.
I remain cold and unmoved,
proving sun unreliable
and time inflexible.
In the chancel, a lamp's red flicker
attempts to tell me I am brittle.
I tear praise from a hymnal,
scrawl across the page:

for circumspect sex, call Mary M on xxx

I leave it on the pew's edge and rise
with nothing old, or new, to confess.

Last Supper with Sarah

I should have skimmed my plate
towards her head,
sliced her open
like a poorly boiled egg.

Watched gobs of glair
drip on her scarf,
glued splinters of shell
to her thin pink scalp.

I should have forked her livered hand
to the starched white linen,
tightened my fist against
smug religion.

Felt her plump flesh
resist the tines, submit
to the bone-scrape
of stainless steel.

I should have yanked the candle
from its silver grasp,
hovered it steady
beneath her chins.

Singed the bristles
of her powdered jowls,
balked at the stench
of foul black welts.

I should have siphoned the fat
from her Boden-clad back,
squeezed reeking tallow
into yellow balls.

Fed her to the sharp beaks
of the territorial
pheasant cocks
strutting on her lawn.

When Sarah said
she'd rather her daughter dead
than queer,

I said
she'd rather be dead
than here.

Spotlight

Sitting in a square of light
you watch me undress,
eyes narrowed by years.

I fix you in crosshairs,
beg an unnamed woe to rest
in the dust between us.

You anchor like a stain
where the sun's daily arc
has faded my fabric.

My heart hammers bone bars;
hunger pounds its fist
on my door;

a thirst, more intimate
than the hush of thaw,
lashes my skin with cuts

no thicker than thread.
I am running and held—
a dog tied to a tree.

Sin Is Due to Open in a Room Above Kitty's

High tide fills clouds with odd light,
captures my collarbones
and softens my throat
white as exposed belly.
I wear blue for luck.

The world rattles my door
with opaque information,
offers my battered life meaning.
I am not significant enough
to be a footnote.

I lick the wounds of truth
with isolation,
tackle loneliness
with easy-access alcohol
to dull the night's toxic industry.

I sober to a new man
in the hot seat.
A rotting carcass who reaps
the benefits of greed
and a hunger for danger.

There is no animal husbandry
in this meat factory.
I am disposable and new.
An emaciated mare
barely good for glue.

Two Things I Know, Father Byrne

I.

The size of the needle's eye
through which I am observed
will remain unchanged

whether I borrow modesty
from a pencil's nib,
or empty my mouth of truths—

so loose
they form candy-floss clouds
above my gunmetal town.

II.

The length of eternity for you—
who stalks the walled grounds,
stark and forlorn—is equal

to that of my lover who leans
in thorn-threaded hedgerows,
naked as winter's larch,

and waits for me to prick
his sensibilities
with the tip of my tongue.

What It Means to Prey

He leans close enough
to agitate the slip
of space between us.
Friction creates heat.
A silent exhale
grazes my hair,
he swells and flares
on the inhale.
He is envious
of the thin blue straps
beneath my black dress;
the ease with which
certain fabrics rip.

He snatches my attention
like a shard of glass
overstepped
in a derelict building.

Later,
he will demonstrate
desire for me
in the cracked ribs
of his current lover,
who walks her house
like the ghost of one
who once lived.

A Thirst for Rain
after Rosemary Tonks

I have lived them, and lived them.

Swollen afternoons of seared skin
when nothing mattered more
than the crow's love of bone
or the damselflies' tangled rise
above idle water.

Powdered nights of smeared facts,
bending to wring a braid of notes
from throats of fat, white cats
who could buy my time
but never the width of my skies.

A Seed Sown

I cradle her by the window.
Copper curls, damp with sleep,
darken the crook of my arm.

I cup her foot in the palm
of my hand, thumb
the estuary of her milk-mouth.

I wonder if she has her father's eyes.
I think of him more than I care to admit,
hear him rustling through leaves outside.

After Work Drinks, Holborn

He releases his interest
like crushed cardamom seeds
gripped in a warm fist.
The scent draws me close
enough to slide a slim palm
across his chest.

He says, *present company
is troublesome luggage.*
It's difficult to swallow
the tight collar of his words,
sharp like the cut of his shirt
against the skin of my dress.

I suck the last
of my bourbon and ice,
step into the warm wall of evening
and slip the ring back on my finger.

Cherries
after Charles Baudelaire

before you nail me in
know what it is
to take your life every night
yet stay alive

> take one quart of rum
> another of gin
> sprig my gums with mint
> rinsed in bitters

write a sugar-syrup
eulogy on strips
of long-gone skin
dashed with lime

> pour me over ice
> smashed like fallen birds
> bury me with a mouth full
> of cherries

New Year

You see:
two women in The Libertine.
Molasses light on crescent cheeks,
plum blush and plump lips,
lucent throats against matt black.

I see:
a still frame of silent violence.
Faces burn with a love that does not exist,
fists clenched, knuckles blanched.
One word too many, a thousand too few.

You see sisters bathed in colour.
I see sisters washed of each other.

The Mistake I Always Make

startles like the pierce
of an injured bird's beak;
rolls like a marble in my mouth,
splinters enamel;
tugs like the river, or a fish
that will not be caught.

But lay an ear
to my boundary fault,
you will not hear the echo
of hollow coalfields
or the black crush
of rock-lined fissures.

I have a pulse:
push through layers,
expose my ribs' curve.
And this time I will listen.

She Is Plotting Against Me

Wearing self-awarded medals
she makes her own pleasure—
a wind-chime in an airtight room;

watches a spider drag a beetle
to a dark crack between rocks.
Shadows tilt in the silent fight.

She commits to memory the colour
of my tea; ties me to a butcher's block;
whets her scissors by lamplight.

I traffic thoughts around regret,
arrive at the edge of an answer:
my hair was long when we first met.

Shaping Words
for R.J.A

Your fingers twitch.
This is how I know
you are asleep.

It brings me close
to honesty
not shared in daylight:

when I wait for the hedge,
thick with noise,
to quieten;

or windfall apples
to soften;
for the time to be right.

Instead, I tell the wet caramel
of the tree's rotting stump
and our white-washed gable

that you draw me
like the flush
bordering a scratch.

Tonight,
I curve to your back
as a hand cups a flame.

The Mathematics of Chance

I do not envy the young their short past.
With unschooled hands in teenage sheets
we explored the curve of skin on spine.
In summer parks, thick with cider,
we leaned as bookends, back to back.

I do not envy the young their lit future.
Gathering years like scattered dice,
We spread the mathematics of chance
upon our bed; gamble with nights
we may not trust the sun to rise.

DNR
i.m. A.J.C

Another night
succumbs to copper.
Morning swallows sentinel light
in the hospital carpark.
Incoming weather is dark.

Flickering lids
journey the geography
of sixty-seven summers,
rest on condensed light,
distant as heather honey.

I blow thirty-two winds
of the mariner's rose
upon cooling skin, slack
like a sail's empty belly.
Life changes tack.

The music of monitors
steps up a pace. A timpani
slows, then holds low C.
I run cold water to drown
the sound of relief.

Glasgow Coma Scale

First on scene, emergency services
score you six and leave without me.
I tail the silence of blue lights,
abandon the car in the ambulance bay.
Trauma team score your four:
pupils not yet fixed. Aggressively cared for
to limit risk of cardiac arrest—
your young organs ready to harvest.

I want to seal my mouth to your dented skull,
suck shape into cranial plates,
ask about the day we lay naked under leaves
tasting the age of rain. Placed bets on when
the lone apple would fall from the winter-bound tree.
You already knew and kept it from me.

Killing Time in the Relatives' Room

It seems clear: only those
with clean soles come in here.
The swamp-green carpet,
peppered dark and bright
like buttered spinach, sucks
against the quicksand
of washable walls.

A framed print stretches
a wooden jetty
across a pallid lake,
reflects a sky that should taste
of ginger's latent heat;
a garden table
strewn with petals
fallen from slumped poppies.

Silent and observational,
a sombre blue bible
offers Good News
beside an empty box of tissues
and an unrung phone.
In this holding bay, news of quitters
arrives quietly on white shoes.

Kintsugi
i.m. A.T.G

     I unhinge
  golden hoops from still-soft lobes
       with the delicacy
    of horology. Curve the memory of her warmth,
vital as a bee's weight,
        through my own ears.
  Careful not to crease the stained sheet
        that hides her wounds
  from neck to navel. My leg, pressed to hers,
     mourns
    the transfer of heat: a red-hulled ship
       ploughing through ice fields,
        sealing the fractures
      with seams
   of gold.

In the School of Life Sciences

Stories from birth
are stored in scars made
with blunt handles
and sharp blades.

I pass specimens
in glass jars.
Pink-painted
plaster casts

of gashed bellies
are peeled to reveal
dead babies
in dead mothers.

Through metal doors
to regimental rows
of steel benches.
I am ready to work.

Plug my lungs,
delay the formalin burn
that numbs my nose,
salts my eyes.

I prise the lid
from a plastic tub,
raise the neck and head
halved last week:

study the tongue
that tasted
the sweetness
of another;

lips that curved words
of bedtimes tales
before purged of blood
and colour.

Orkney
after Andrew Greig

In this time between
bare branch and flower,
thorns still soft on the stalk,
we idle between tides
in the needle-shadow
of St Peter's tower.

Sun drips low, lengthens
sloped gravestones.
We sit on blistered,
wind-splintered wood
in a rowing boat
banked on dry sand.

Evening darkens in waves.
We empty hipflasks,
fill our mouths with freedom,
list with our shifting cargo
of laughter—undisciplined
as dog rose through hedgerow.

I press fingertips to flesh,
feel you beat against bone.
Love's undertow
sucks you out to sea
in a rush of spindrift and foam,
knows to return you to me.

I Was Once a Girl in a Fountain, Splashing a Boy

My day is empty of all but time.
I disperse old anxieties,
push blue through layers of grey;
insist like thin sun through cloud
or an elbow through timeworn wool.

I sharpen my gaze
on the surface of the bay,
consider the violence
of waves thrust upon canvas
or words scratched on paper.

October light pulses the river,
reddens a single rosehip
on a leafless branch, whips
the western sky
to a sugared-cream shine.

The water's edge rushes
like the open mouth of a story—
all gush and foam—interrupts
a thought built from small bits of silence:
blood will slow and thicken in eddies
when I am least ready.

About the Author

Morag Anderson is an emerging Scottish poet based in Highland Perthshire. Her work explores human connections—concealed violence, love, and everything in between. She has been published widely in literary journals and anthologies. She was placed in The Blue Nib Chapbook VI Contest, shortlisted for the Bridport Poetry Prize, and won Over the Edge New Poet. She is a member of the writing collective Poets Abroad.

Fly on the Wall Press

A publisher with a conscience.
Publishing high quality stories, poetry and anthologies on pressing issues, from exceptional writers around the globe. Founded in 2018 by founding editor, Isabelle Kenyon.

Other publications:

Please Hear What I'm Not Saying
Persona Non Grata
Bad Mommy / Stay Mommy by Elisabeth Horan
The Woman With An Owl Tattoo by Anne Walsh Donnelly
the sea refuses no river by Bethany Rivers
White Light White Peak by Simon Corble
Second Life by Karl Tearney
The Dogs of Humanity by Colin Dardis
Small Press Publishing: The Dos and Don'ts by Isabelle Kenyon
Alcoholic Betty by Elisabeth Horan
Awakening by Sam Love
Grenade Genie by Tom McColl
House of Weeds by Amy Kean and Jack Wallington
No Home In This World by Kevin Crowe
The Goddess of Macau by Graeme Hall
The Prettyboys of Gangster Town by Martin Grey
The Sound of the Earth Singing to Herself by Ricky Ray
Inherent by Lucia Orellana Damacela
Medusa Retold by Sarah Wallis
Pigskin by David Hartley
We Are All Somebody
Aftereffects by Jiye Lee
Someone Is Missing Me by Tina Tamsho-Thomas
In Conversation with Small Press Publishers
PowerPoint Eulogy by Mark Wilson

Odd as F*ck by Anne Walsh Donnelly
Muscle and Mouth by Louise Finnigan
Modern Medicine by Lucy Hurst
These Mothers of Gods by Rachel Bower

Social Media:

@fly_press (Twitter)
@flyonthewall_poetry (Instagram)
@flyonthewallpress (Facebook)
www.flyonthewallpress.co.uk

www.ingramcontent.com/pod-product-compliance
Lightning Source LLC
LaVergne TN
LVHW092101060526
838201LV00047B/1519